Beyond All Galaxies

Poetry and Reflections for the Journey

About The Author

Born in 1937 in the Pacific Northwest and for 66 years a Sister of St. Joseph of Peace, Kathleen currently lives in community in Seattle, Washington. Over the years she has served in many ministries: Education, Social Services, Boards of Directors for Healthcare, Province/Region and Congregation leadership, wilderness retreats in the Canadian Okanagan mountains and as a spiritual director. She served as vice-president of Pax Christi International for ten years and for three years in the presidency of LCWR. She holds advanced degrees in history and social work and is a Zen teacher. When asked the questions: "A Zen teacher? How does this fit with being Catholic and a member of a religious congregation?" She responded, "When I decided to take up Zen, I had also decided that, if I were to do that, I would want three conditions: I would find a teacher who understands Catholicism, who understands religious life, and who knows authentic Zen practice. I was fortunate to find in Joan Rieck a teacher who understands all three. I studied with her for 30 years.

In 2007, Kathleen was given authorization to teach Zen by Yamada Ryôun Roshi, the Abbot of Sanbo Zen Zendo in Kamakura, Japan. In the words of the Abbot's father Koun Yamada Roshi, "One does not have to be Buddhist to practice Zen. The practice of Zen makes you better what you are." Kathleen has found this to be so.

Believing in the omnipresence of the Mystery, named by many names, her spirituality is deeply grounded in and shaped by the beauty and oneness of all Creation, the Infinite Mystery hidden in plain sight.

Beyond All Galaxies

Poetry and Reflections for the Journey

Kathleen Pruitt, CSJP

Kenmare Press
2023

Cover art: Sister Carol Sachse, OCD

Watercolor paintings: Sister Julie Codd, CSJP

Cover design and book layout: Cristina Turino

First Printing: 2023

ISBN: 979-8-9876403-0-2

eISBN: 979-8-9876403-1-9

Library of Congress Control Number: 2023908469

Kenmare Press
399 Hudson Terrace
Englewood Cliffs, NJ 07632
www.csjp.org/kenmarepress

This book is dedicated to the memory of
Sister Louise Du Mont, CSJP and Sister Elizabeth Ann Brennan, CSJP
each of whom shaped and shared my life in special ways.

Contents

Preface

This little book of poems and reflections is one person's growing awareness of the all-pervading *Mystery* named by many names – *God, Love, Infinite Absolute, Ground of All Being, Source of All Life, Emptiness.* As is true of *Mystery*, it is beyond comprehension, conceptualization, and intellectualization, so often it is approached through simile and metaphor allowing us to make connections, comparisons, and descriptions. The poems in this collection are my attempt to give expression to a *Mystery* so near to us yet, sometimes, seemingly so far away, shown forth in all creation. Each person's spiritual journey into *Mystery* takes its own course, but there is a common desire to give expression to an experience of the incomprehensible closer to us than we are to ourselves. I hope that my attempt at describing this journey will encourage others to give voice to what is, in so many ways, the deepest restless longing of the human heart. I hope you will enjoy the poems, and, if you have not already done so, write your own!

Each of the seven sections in this book includes six or seven poems written in various places all over the world, inspired by the mountains of Canada, the eruption of Mount St. Helens in Washington state, the Sonnenhof Zen Center in Germany, the temples of Japan, the desert lands of the American Southwest, and encounter with Creation everywhere. In addition, you will find several brief reflections based on the wisdom of Jesus, Meister Eckhart, Hildegard of Bingen, Julian of Norwich, John of the Cross, Thomas Merton, and Zen Master Dōgen Zenji, Yamada Koun Roshi, and others. Each brief reflection is an edited version of a longer reflection prepared each week for a contemplative prayer group that I lead at St. Mary-on-the-Lake and online.

Acknowledgements

Art is another form of poetry and the artist a poet. The cover of this book is an original painting created by Carol Sachse, OCD, a member of the Carmel of Reno in Nevada. The watercolors at the beginning of each section of the book are the work of Julie Codd, CSJP, member of the Congregation of the Sisters of St. Joseph of Peace. I thank them both for adding their poetry-in-art to this book. I want to also thank Jan Linley for her counsel, encouragement, and for editing of the reflections. Thanks, too, to Cristina Turino for layout and overall meticulous attention to detail in finalizing this work.

Those of us who take halting steps attempting to articulate *Infinite Mystery* in poetic imagery are often shy about sharing these articulations. One may agree to do that sharing only at the invitation and encouragement of others. I am one who has been blessed by the urgings of others to share some of what I've written over a lifetime in this tiny book of poems and reflections. I want to thank a few here: Sheila Lemieux, CSJP, then Congregation Leader, who called several years ago asking if I would consider sharing some of my reflections; the Carmelite Sisters in Reno, Nevada, who so generously give of their sacred space and loving presence; and in particular to those in the community who have journeyed with me. Special thanks to Claire Sokol, OCD, a spiritual guide for me for nearly 20 years, my heartfelt gratitude, and to Ann Weber, OCD, and Susan Weber, OCD. To Joan Rieck, my Zen Teacher and guide for nearly 35 years, a profound bow. And last but certainly not least, my deep gratitude goes to the Congregation of the Sisters of St. Joseph of Peace—*my friends and sisters*—who in so many ways have opened space for me to be who I am and to become who I say I want to be.

Winds and Oceans

Air we breathe: Breath of Spirit, oceans swell tides and wave governed by the moon. Air and ocean: womb and pulse of life! Breathe in/breathe out: one breath of the universe.

Shaft of sunlight
pierces gray cloud
The rain falls softly
upon the wind

        Wind blows briskly
        Waves tumble one upon the other
        Sandy shore awaits them both

Wet and windy
Rain walks lightly on the roof
Wind cries softly in the trees

Always Becoming

Mystery in the universe thundering in the roaring wave
breathing gently in the sighing wind
giving life in rain that gentles seed to grow
bringing death in heat of broiling sun that parches waiting earth.
Mystery in the universe that flings myriad of stars
drops down stardust to form and people and creature all the land.
O Mystery teeming, boiling, bubbling, bursting
with life and energy… drawing, lifting, plunging, carrying, holding
all that is:
Just This! This extraordinary ordinary moment!
A grain of sand, a teardrop in the eye. O Mystery beyond
all understanding — I bend in humbled awe.

A Mighty Wind

You, mighty gusting wind
  move me as a leaf tossed
  across a barren land;
Lift me – lift me up on some far off
  mountain top to stand.
Leave me there to ponder
  your vast reaches; and there to hear
  your breath. It blows, it whips, it whispers
  going freely where it will.
Touching lightly now, then running fast
  and strong before.
Circling back upon yourself you dance
  atop the trees
and at the same time whirl earth's sands
  around my knees.
You play, you chase, you tease!
  Then lay in stillness I know not where
  till gusts of gentle playfulness toss about my hair!
Oh yes, please leave me on this mountain top
  where I can stand alone
knowing in its emptiness that I really am alone.

Impermanence

The rushing sea washes over, covering me
with tangy brine, throwing
foamy curtains at the water's edge
then drawing back quickly lest
they be seen as permanent.
Here there is nothing permanent.
Deep blue yields to jade-green
and then to slate blue-black.
Footprints marked upon the sand
by gull or child or dog leave
no trace as sea smooths out its space.
Tall castles, moats and walls crafted carefully
offer no resistance to crashing wave and biting sea.
Instead they fall helplessly before water's relentless siege.
On a distant rise, naked twisted trees stand
sentinel to wind-force as harsh as it can be gentle.
Sands shift in ever-changing patterns
as unseen wind sweeps and twists – now dancing, now still.
Clouds move across the sky – an artist's hand
changing colors in the sea; sun slips
through here and there like a finishing brush
leaving but a touch or pool of light, and then dark again.
Here there is nothing permanent.

Searching

Winds leap and swirl
in what seems a mighty effort to find a resting place.
Then sit in a moment of calm
amid branches of the taller trees.
But not for long.
Like the soul at thirst for the living God,
Stretching, searching, seeking – it lifts again.
In constant motion it defies the moment –
as if the Spirit lifts its voice to say I AM and I
breathe where I will. It is yours but to follow.
Come! Dance with me, fleet afoot along the shore
or floating high amid the trees, or resting for a quiet moment
to hear the deep-down hidden silence.
I am all of these. Hear me and be refreshed.

For Reflection: An Exercise in Seeing and Listening

Take a few minutes during the day or early evening before it gets dark to go outside. If you can't go outside find the biggest window in your home and view the outside from there. Spend five or six minutes just looking—barren trees, evergreen bushes, birds, puppies, kitties, grass, weeds, mountains, rivers, lakes, clouds—just look, long lingering, reflective looking. Slowly, let your gaze move from tree to tree, from bush to cloud. What do you see? If you feel so inclined, jot down what you experienced, note similarities or differences, if there are any, between simply looking and actually seeing.

Now, close your eyes, stand or sit as motionless and as silent as possible. Spend five or six minutes just listening to rustling breezes or wind, traffic, voices, airplanes. What do you hear? If you are so inclined, jot down what you experienced, note similarities or differences, if there are any, between how you ordinarily hear and your reflective intentional listening.

You can do this same reflective exercise using the other three senses: taste, smell, and touch. The wonderful, precious gifts of the five senses are incredible windows into so much. Without them our intellectual, conceptual, and other dimensions of encounter would be one or two dimensional, instead of the rich multi-faceted, multi-dimensional reality we experience. It is possible that we take our senses for granted! Take a moment to reflect upon and give thanks that we "are so fearfully and wonderfully made."

Try to apply this exercise to your contemplative practice. Sitting is an important and wonderful opportunity to attentively gaze and draw into the sacred space of deep silence, gently acknowledging thoughts that arise, sounds that we hear and, with equal gentleness, letting them go, returning to the rhythmic breathing in, breathing out until even that falls away and we just sit, light sitting in light.

Autumn Winds

There's wisdom in the autumn winds
whispering now of coming changes.
Trees often first to feel begin to let go.
Leaves turn from green to red and gold, so beginning
life's descent to winter's waiting rest.
Soon the trees will barren be, life-sap dropping
to source and earth.
It seems that death will have its way, yet
lifeforce sleeps in restful pose
to rise and green another day.
Thinking of wisdom in autumn winds
whispering softly of coming changes.
What is it I must let go – what colors will I show
as life drops to source and earth?
It seems that death will have its way, yet
life will sleep in restful pose
to rise and live in Love's embrace.

Does the Ocean Meditate

I think the ocean meditates!
It sits within a vast, silent depth of itself,
yet at its surface in rhythmic, pulsating
constancy breathes out and in coming to the shore
then drawing back into itself only to repeat
this constant breathing out and in
until it reaches fullness of its destination.
I think the ocean meditates.

Autumn Day at Ocean's Edge

The soft edges of this summer day
move wistfully into open arms of Autumn,
whose breath, gentle in its caress, invites
green leaves, gilded gold and red,
to loosen their grip and flutter downward,
reminders of changes yet to come.
Far offshore a wispy
fog hovers, like lingering smoke of summer fires,
making ocean waves gleam pewter-gray in
movement to this pebbled beach,
where spindly-legged pipers
peck their way to meet
approaching surf then
retreat hastily to avoid its chilly fingers.
Advance, retreat, they come and go in
perfect rhythm with ocean's ebb and flow –
what am I to know as I merge with this mesmerizing show?

At Play

Midnight blue to jade green
crested white upon the wave.
Over and over, wave upon wave
the ocean calls and beckons.
What is it that so holds the eye
drawing heart to follow to mark of pounding surf.
Then surely as the drawing sound
sight will clouded be as
fog-fingers flit across the sand
wrapping in a ghostly hand all within its way.
So quickly hid, so quickly to emerge
as, swept away, the fog moves on and
once again the eye can see.
Sand gives up itself
to force of gusting wind propelled
along the shore to unknown place of rest –
and once there to be picked up
and moved again.
Shaped and reshaped from
small mound to mighty dune.
Rolling, dipping, desert-like, mile-upon-mile,
how many grains are gathered here…
to the eye each too small to see
and yet, when come together
they an awesome presence be.
So too unseen breath does blow
propelling each along a way
to ever ending and beginning
from dark to blazing day.

For Reflection: Sink into Silence

Sink, sink, sink into silence...
Still, still sounds that surround.
Soften, soften sinews that stay me.
Silence, silence – find silence in sound.

As you prepare to sit, holding within the Great Mystery of Love, take a few moments to call to mind three attitudes so necessary to practice:

- Great faith – Faith that we, and all beings, are already One in the Great Mystery of Love. It is coming to realize our true self as the Oneness we always are and have been in the Great Mystery we can never grasp with our intellect and understanding. We come to know without knowing, sometimes swiftly, sometimes slowly. Be still and know.

- Great doubt – Sink into the silence with no expectations, no clinging, no demands, no achievements, no images, no words, only the restless longing deep within. Listen.

- Great determination – Don't give up! No matter how hard, no matter if the time seems vacant and dry like nothing is happening. Don't give up! We are already one. The door of realization opens sometimes slowly, unannounced, sometimes in brief glimpses, aha moments; sometimes it is overpowering. Remember, let go of expectations. Let images, words, thoughts drop away. Be still. Listen.

When we enter into contemplative/meditative silence, open and attentive, without our knowing it, we are imperceptibly changed. We are opened to see differently, hear differently, act differently. Compassion and mercy, hope and courage, gentleness and justice are strengthened. And through our hands, our hearts, our words, our actions, we can more tenderly touch ourselves and those near to and far from us: the wounded, the broken, those who rejoice and those who mourn. We participate in the healing and wholeness of this wonderful, wounded world, one breath, one word, one action at a time!

Open, open, open into silence...
Still, still sounds that surround.
Soften, soften sinews that stay me.
Silence, silence – find silence in sound.

Streams and Rivers

Rivers gather strength from small beginnings: raindrops feed trickles, trickles become streams, streams merge together becoming rivers. Lakes are fed by rivers and streams. Rivers find a way to oceans. Clouds reclaim water from the earth's lakes and oceans, and raindrops fall again.

Waterfall singing
Silence in the garden
Words among friends are quiet

Swiftly passing clouds
Dark with raindrops falling.
Who is it that feels the splash?
Oceans giving and receiving are the same

A rushing stream
Darkness of night
Cool breeze through open window

Toward Mighty Seas

I race with special urgency along this narrow course
toward mighty seas and distant oceans
to destinations yet unknown even in my haste.
I come from lakes and mountain streams.
Snowmelt, ice, and gentle rains make up my substance.
I flow and in my flowing find
both depths and shallows
for my soul to swell.
Deep down my heart's hope finds expression
in my longing to be free – to find
a promised fullness,
lost in the NOW of an eternal destiny.

Shadows in the Mist

Mist, a ghostly presence shrouds
from sight what lies beyond
lifting now and then allowing
glimpse of what heart knows but eye cannot see.
Like a veil, this misty curtain separating
time from vast eternity.
Fleeting shadow of what is there
assures the pilgrims step by conscious step
though it seems the mist luring onward
but shrouding still what lies beyond –
lifting now and then allowing
a glimpse of what heart knows but eye cannot see.

The Sea Calls

Call of the Sea draws me
and so I walk the distance to
its noisy moving edge,
hoping I think to learn something new
but only ancient whispers do I hear.
It comes, moving slowly from some far-off shore.
It retreats without care for who would
hold it here in place.

There is wisdom in its coming and its going
governed only by the rhythm of the universe.
It does not cling to the shore from which it left
nor to the shore it reaches.

And so my life – is it governed by rhythm
of the universe? Free to come and free to go –
not clinging to any shore but responsive to
the ancient pull that draws but does not bind.

I hoped at water's edge to learn something new
but only ancient whispers do I hear.
Ever ancient, ever new – and it is enough.

For Reflection: Invitations to Transforming C

The following piece of evocative wisdom was shared t,
happens to be my Zen teacher. It echoes what we are invited to reflec, ,
by so many of the spiritual guides, teachers, companions, great sages, and
saints. Sometimes hearing the same message in another way is helpful in
prompting deeper reflection on things we already know somewhere deep
within.

> *People everywhere try so hard to make the world better. Their*
> *intentions are admirable, yet they seek to change everything but*
> *themselves. To make yourself a better person is to make the world*
> *a better place. Who develops industries that fill the air and water*
> *with toxic waste? How did we humans become immune to the*
> *plight of refugees, or hardened to the suffering of animals raised*
> *to be slaughtered? Until we transform ourselves, we are like mobs*
> *of angry people screaming for peace. In order to move the world,*
> *we must be able to stand still in it. Now more than ever, I place*
> *my faith in Gandhi's approach: Be the change you wish to see in*
> the world. *Nothing is more essential for the twenty-first century*
> *and beyond than personal transformation. It's our only hope.*
> *Transforming ourselves is transforming the world.*
>
> Yongey Mingyur Rinpoche

We are familiar with biblical passages like *Love your neighbor as you*
love yourself; Do unto others as you would have done to you; We are our
sisters' and brothers' keepers; and *What I do to another I do to myself.* These
and many others are invitations to look deeply and listen attentively,
invitations to be open to transforming grace. To allow ourselves to be
moved—transformed even—Mingyur Rinpoche's words remind us again
that time in meditation is a time for standing still. It is a time for listening
with the ear of the heart, a time for opening to the transforming presence
of a Mystery of Love within, a Mystery closer to us than we are to ourselves,
a Mystery we cannot comprehend but can trust is transforming. Jesus
knew this, so did the Buddha, so have the saints and sages of all times
whose lives and living offer us pathways to the deepest longings of our very
being. And the restless longings of our own hearts tell us that we, too, know
this.

May the words offered by so many be a gentle catalyst for each of us to look deeply into ourselves and see if there is anything, no matter how small, that we long to do to be ever more open to the great Mystery closer to us than we are to ourselves. Are we holding back in any way from being the change we wish to see in the world? Can we be thankful for the opportunity, the freedom, to stand still in it and so help transform our wonderful, wounded world?

I, a River

Rushing, rolling, sweeping, swirling, swelling
I make haste to unknown places.
High above me I hear the drone of a mighty jet.
It too makes way to other places,
places named which change from day to day.

How different for me – I'm bound by a laid-out course
and cannot change save with years,
perhaps thousands long, of patient wearing down,
unless disturbed by some cataclysmic change in
Mother Earth which rousts me from my bed.

And so I go, onward to a nameless sea. But in
my course will join so many others
losing my identity in theirs, yet in the loss
gaining more in strength and grandeur.
I proceed in measured course
until at last I come to where I'm meant to be.

Where Do the Raindrops Go

I wonder! I wonder
where the raindrops go?
Bouncing off the tarp, falling
to a floor of soft pine needles.
Where does the water go?
Already soaked earth
unable to absorb the
wet abundance –
It sits in small reflecting puddles
or cuts a winding path through duff
and meanders down the slope.
But where do the raindrops go?
Are they hopeful and expectant
to join again the great oceans?
Or do they only wish to find a stream or lake?
Or even more do they long
to tell me that I too
am but a drop of rain –
a piece of earth weeping,
wending, joyfully joining.
I am the rain!

Ancient Patterns

The touch of ocean on the sand
draws patterns filled with
mystery always changing, etched
by water against a rock or shell
or just the sand itself.
And somewhere far from ocean's shore
an old Tibetan Monk or Holy Navajo
etches life's mysteries in sand
that once read and blessed will to the sand
and sea again be given.

For Reflection: The Journey Is Worth Beginning

As you begin to meditate, refresh yourself in heart, mind and body and notice how you come to this very sacred time. How we experience our whole day with all its comings and goings, ups and downs, hopes and aspirations is in very real ways also prayer.

It is important that we remind ourselves we live, move, and have our being always in the One and are one with the Source of Life. Our journey in prayer is a journey opening us to realization and experience of this Mystery we cannot grasp intellectually. Sometimes the journey seems dark and difficult. Sometimes the journey seems filled with light and assuring feelings of peace and promise, hope and glimpses of grace. Sometimes the journey is hard, seems impossible, and it is difficult to say much at all about what is taking place. There may even be a nagging little voice that says, "Why am I doing this at all? It's too hard and I'm tired of trying."

Any journey has its ups and downs and sometimes it's important on the journey to ask for help, guidance, or direction. The same is true of the spiritual journey we are on, being opened to the realization and experience of the Infinite Mystery we cannot grasp intellectually is not always straightforward or clear. It's good for us as journeyers to periodically check in with a trusted guide or teacher who can help us see, hear more clearly, or be assured, offer helpful insight, or suggest different pathways.

It is equally important that we don't judge progress or what we perceive as little or no progress in our meditative/contemplative journey. We are all, and always will be, humble beginners cultivating an attitude of openness, attentiveness, reverence, trust, joy, and child-like expectation coming from a deep heart-longing.

Have faith that what we desire is already within and that the Infinite Mystery is closer to us than we are to ourselves. It is not beyond, across the vast sea, or high up in the sky … No! The Mystery we name Love is very near, already one with our very being, there for us to know without knowing this wondrous grace. When doubt or questions arise, cling to that deep faith. Be persistent and patient; don't give up! The journey is worth beginning and beginning again and again to be moved from where we are to where we might not otherwise go, to a place we do not know. This is subtle, imperceptible, but so real that without knowing it we are being transformed; it is God's work in us.

Julian of Norwich spoke of the Love that is flowing through the universe and that holds us all and will not let us go; It is ours to realize and experience. It is Infinite Mystery revealing Itself everywhere, in the good, the beautiful, the not so good and even the dark where Love weeps. See in faith. Listen with the ear of the heart. Be compassionate as Love is compassionate.

God will come to you much sooner
If you will but stay completely still
Instead of searching for God wildly
Till body and soul fall ill.

God is pure emptiness
Not touched by now and here;
The more you strive to reach God, the
Further God recedes.

Angelus Silesius

Gentle Rain

I feel the rain in tiny drops
upon my upturned face.
Enough to say 'sufficient is the
water of my grace.'
Don't miss what is before you
to see, to touch, to feel, to taste
for in this moment only, Love
is given and is graced.

Etchings in the Sand

Wind etchings in the sand
like ancient villages uncovered
to be seen and then to change again.
What distant shore, last touched
hastens you away, till your white horses
at full gallop atop the crested wave
touch this shore?
What eyes last looked on you
in some far-off place,
scanned horizon as now I do
in awe and wonder at the mystery
which drives your
ebb and flow, held hostage
to this constant motion
yet freer than I'll ever be
to come and go.

The Well Is Deep

There is a well I often sit by.
When I look down it is deep and
its waters are still.
Sometimes when the light is right
I see clearly. The still waters
reflect back to me the image of my face.
Strange it seems, but in the stillness of the
water, looking into my own reflected eyes I
catch a glimpse of soul – Spirit deep and quiet.
When it is dark, and often it is, the water
seems invisible … so I drop a pebble – perhaps it's just
a thought. But in the quiet of that moment
I hear a sound of silent presence.
Believing, in the darkness, I let down my cup
and drink deeply. Refreshed, cleansed, cleared!
In this living water I see differently.

For Reflection: The Crack in the Heart

As you prepare to sit, contemplate a saying drawn from ancient Sufi wisdom that calls us to renewed awareness. "It is through the crack in our heart that the Mystery enters."

Contemplation is spoken about in different words by many different people, in many different spiritual traditions. Each of us ponders its meaning for ourselves. However, pondering and words spoken are not the essentials. So, what is essential? Simply defined, contemplation, as we use the term, means to gaze attentively, to make space for listening with the ear of the heart, and to listen without expectation or clinging.

I like to think of this attentive gazing, this unencumbered listening, as in the words of a Sufi Mystic, the crack in our heart through which the Mystery enters, or better yet, the crack in our heart through which we enter the Mystery becoming one with it. Through this experience we open ourselves to be emptied of thought and concepts about self, God, absolute infinite, holiness, enlightenment and more. Through our making space for attentive gazing and unencumbered listening, we come to experience, sometimes slowly, sometimes quickly, stillness, letting go, letting be.

It is in this contemplative/meditative silence that somehow, eventually, essentially, we come to see differently, hear differently, know differently, experience differently, and act differently. As you sit and enter the Mystery through the crack in your heart, believe it to be a deep and mysterious truth, knowing that as we allow ourselves to be transformed in the silence of contemplation, we are allowing Love in and through us to transform our world. This is the power of contemplative presence, never for ourselves alone, but flowing out in compassion, mercy, self-giving love, and caring for all beings.

Songs of the Universe

Our universe billions of years old -- ever ancient, ever new! Birthing anew, in timeless creativity yet intimately close in each measured moment – look up, look around -- listen to the universe singing!

Light dawns
Day born anew
Music of the universe plays in harmony

> The universe a grain of rice
> A drop of water all the seas
> All light in but a spark
> So It is – So It is!

Sunrays of light
Beauty spreads the earth
Wrapping all in rainbow colors

The Universe Sings

Who is it that renders me mute
    in the vastness of such wonder —
Silence feeds my spirit! It nurtures
    the very life that breathes
    within and out.
There is no muse to speak a word
    nor artist to splash a kaleidoscope of
    color - no bard to form a song, or
    harpist to strum a note as prelude
    to earth's great symphony.
Yet in this sounding silence all sound
    merges becoming one - A swelling symphony.
Listen with your heart: The Universe is singing!

Morning Chill Calls

Freshness dances on the morning chill...
See droplets of rain hang frozen from the leaves
like diamond beads strung to catch the morning sun.
Birdsongs sung in cacophonous harmony
wake sleeping earth to the newness of the day.
Sweet scent of desert perfume pleasing
    senses of the passerby ... calling in the silence for a moment's
    notice.
Embraced by mothering arms of snow-clad mountains
there is a joyfulness about the earth
    rich-ringing with the grace of rain;
springing sprightly with promise of new life.
What is there in the sounding-silence
    of this place that captivates the heart,
    revealing in its fullness an emptying of grace.
There is the deepest freshness in the morning chill.

Stars Call to Life

Ah bright stars resplendent above
the darkened earth –
tossed with careless glee
by one who takes delight in
radiant twinkling, tinkling crystal –
silent music across the night sky.
One who laughs at shimmering
ringing silence
calling the moon to dance upon
the waters of the earth.
The breath of infinite laughter
shakes the trees
moves the clouds and draws
fiery chariot of the sun into
heaven's span – stars and moon
for a time out-brillianced
in dazzling rays of
warmth and light.
And what of earth as she
stretches into life, shaking
off refreshing chill of night
making ready for the newness of the day.

For Reflection: Everything Is Your Life

Moments of sitting are moments of gift and grace, and as such, are treasured time in life. Thirteenth-century Zen master Dōgen reminds us:

> Everything is your life. Whatever you encounter, day and night, is your life; you should therefore give yourself to each situation as it arises from moment to moment. Use your life energy toward that purpose, so that from the circumstances that befall you, you may create a harmonious life with all things in their rightful place.

This reminder of the importance of each moment is certainly not foreign to us. Many saints and sages, past and present, from many spiritual traditions urge us to live fully present to each moment, to be mindful, to be aware of the steps we take, to fully engage the task at hand, to live each moment as though it were our last, and to know the present moment is truly the only moment there is. Live it fully for it contains the past, which is gone, and the unfolding future yet to be.

Living fully present to the present moment is an important practice, as are the moments of silence and solitude of contemplation/meditation. Each is an invitation to awareness, an invitation to be present, an invitation to listen deeply with the ear of the heart and to see with the eye of the heart. Living fully present to the present moment is not easy. It is a life journey. Practice presence to the present moment. Don't get discouraged when you find that the mind jumps to something other than what is in this moment. When we find the mind wandering during the silence of contemplation/meditation, acknowledge the wandering and gently return to the breath.

The practice of living into the present moment with intention has its practical gains. It helps us be clearer, more efficient, and often you will get more done with greater ease. Practice of presence to and in the present moment is a gift you can give yourself. In the giving of that gift, you will be nurturing, almost without knowing, an interior silence into which you will almost unconsciously enter.

Now, in the moment of your sitting, be present. Let silence open the space to hear with the ear of your heart. Be still and know that Love, the only name fitting the One we name God, the Ground of you, of me, of all creation, is oneness, not separate. Know without knowing the Ground of your true self.

We shall never rest, until we become that which, in God, we have always been. Meister Eckhart

Waking Up!

Tight clasped fingers of night's darkness
yield their grip to dawn's inbreaking
of a new day.
Early morning wisps of mist
cloak the hills in ever changing robes of majesty.
Earth awakens once again to
the wonder of itself
and calls all creatures great and small
to join the joyful dance.

One with All

I am One with you O Life Force
God of Universe – all Creation!
Daughter spun of stardust,
sun and moonbeam brilliance.
Planted here in earth's own womb –
soil watered by rain and snow,
graced by dew and crystal ice.
A graceful supple tree
bending in unceasing wind –
gentled in the breeze that blows,
made strong in mountain air
and thunderstorm.
Raised to full stature in the fruits of earth
and One with all that is – I AM!
Oceanwide and universal seas beyond.
Endless sky and universe – galaxies, yet unknown,
dark abyss so filled with surging Life Force.

Where Are You?

'Where ARE You?' I asked
then silenced to listen!
Both Joyful and jarring
here's what I heard:

I Am twinkling star in darkened sky
… universe of wonder vast and high

I Am laughter in the playful breeze
… gentle sighing in wind-bent trees.

I Am music in the water's fall
… clear sweet note in all birds' call.

I Am varied beauty of mountain height
… silence in each valley's night.

I Am hurried bustle on city streets
… weeping in lonely heart that beats.

I Am hand out-reaching ever so softly
… in mind-thought simple or lofty.

I Am warm hug of friends embrace
… comfort, caressing — moments of grace.

I Am prayer-filled protest pleading for peace
… working for justice unwilling to cease.

I Am mercy to all — to all freely given
… to the fierce, the frantic, the fearful, the driven.

I'm in palace, in home, in junky motel
… in each precious life whether heaven or hell.

I listened intently, a little afraid
… open to seeing, daring to hear — then
    LOVE simply asked: 'Where NOW are you?
    … for wherever you are I am there too.'

Evening Prayer

Fading o'er horizon's edge
the dying sun streaks with gold
the shores, and catches
in its shimmering light
uplifted branches stretched
out in silent prayer —
as arms embracing all the earth
and stretching even further
to take in the heavens too.
Not satisfied to be silent
the wind breathes whispers
through the shadowed leaves
thus giving sound to mute reverence
that would cry out in praise of glory!

For Reflection: You Already Are What You Seek

As you prepare for this time of silence/presence, take a deep breath and recall the words of Hildegard of Bingen, "Breathing in and breathing out the one breath of the Universe." Think about the wonderful pictures of the universe that are available to us through the eye of the James Webb Space Telescope. They are awe-inspiring glimpses of our 13.8-billion-year-old universe, with more images still to come. We stand within and are part of this ancient universe, this great Mystery, marveling in wonder: *Who am I? Where do I come from? Why am I here? Where do I go?* Whisper these questions as you enter the silence. Be still and know without knowing.

What each of us is invited to realize is not hidden from us, neither is it far from us.

> *Who shall go up for us to heaven, and bring it unto us, that we may hear it, and do it? Neither is it beyond the sea, that we should say, 'Who will go over the sea for me and bring it to me that I may hear it and do it? It is very near to me, in my mouth and in my heart.* (Adapted from the Book of Deuteronomy 30:12-14)

Read those words again slowly. What you come to know without knowing is who you already are, sometimes with a fleeting sense, often when it seems like nothing is happening. You may even doubt. Draw then on great faith. The Infinite Mystery of Love is closer to you than you are to yourself. Be persistent. Give over thought, concepts, descriptions about who you think you are, who you think the other is, who you think God is, and what you think the world is. Let Go. Let Be. Sink into the silence. Let In. Listen to the sound in silence. You already are what you seek; you already are what you long for. Listen. Don't harbor expectations; don't cling to the words of others; don't get stuck in looking for what cannot be seen or visualized. Be still and know. Be awake. Be aware. Be attentive. Listen with the ear of your heart! *Breathing in and breathing out, the one breath of the Universe.*

Silence Speaks So Loudly

Silence, if we but listen deeply, whispers and sings, calling us to deeper places. Sometimes dark, yet light-infused! Be still and know: Mystery beyond all names!

The gong shivers to silence…
　　Silence … silence … silence.
Yes! Clear sweet bird song

　　　　　Surrounded by sound
　　　　　Silence within –
　　　　　　　Is there difference here?

Silence … sound
Sound … silence
One holds the other in cupped ear.

Sounds of Silence

There is a silence here profound beyond words,
    broken only by the whirr of wind that
    in its blowing rustles through leaves and branches
    of this bush and tree.
What speaks to me I do not know, but something stirs
    and in its stirring waters the dryness of my spirit.
I watch the raven, wings outspread, riding lazily
    listlessly upon the wind – unpredictable in its
    coming and going. And somewhere inside
    I feel a desire to ride the wind – free of all except to go
    where air's current should take me.
There is an awesome mystery here that touches deep within.
    It defies name and eludes any permanent feature – no icon,
    no image. Only a pervasive presence unseen, unknown
    yet possessing in its penetrating, pervasive, persistent presence.
There is nothing …. nothing to name in the empty silence
    of my inner space – nothing I dare hold or speak save
    a restlessness of grace.
There is no muse to shape my word; no spark to stir a flame –
    only empty silence and a vast, vast empty space.

From Sound to Silence

Gong struck in measured stroke—
Silence splits the ear
What else is there to hear?
No-thing, all things – below
Above, beyond – in that measured stroke.

Tiny Space Between

There is but a tiny space between
    sound and silence.
Interesting to me is what I name
    as intrusion and what of sound
    is solitude in motion.
Laughter of men at play, a game
    upon the sand, may seem
    an annoyance while pounding
    surf and cry of far-off gull is
    heard as rhythm of the universe.
Is there really difference or is
    the seeming separation distinction
    of my own uncentered making?
What of sound is silence; what of
    Silence sounding is the universe at play?

For Reflection: In Silence

When you step outside or look through your window, reflect on this short offering by Thomas Merton from his poem, "In Silence." Merton calls us to see the whole of creation, ourselves included, as a burning bush.

> ... *The whole*
> *World is secretly on fire. The stones*
> *Burn, even the stones*
> *They burn me. How can a man be still or*
> *Listen to all things burning? How can he dare*
> *To sit with them when*
> *All their silence*
> *Is on fire?*

In *Christian Mystics: 365 Readings and Meditations*, Matthew Fox interprets Merton's poem in the following way:

> *Merton sees into the stones and how they, like the rest of creation, are on fire. He has learned this truth from sitting still and listening "to all things burning." He has learned this lesson from silence. Even the silence burns. The fire of stones speaks to his fire, for they burn him. This language of burning may be another way of speaking about encountering the Cosmic Christ, the light in all things. Light burns. To say "the whole world is secretly on fire" conjures up Moses' experience of God in the burning bush. Every bush is a burning bush — this we now know from today's science. Every bush, all matter, contains photons or light waves, which in theological language might represent the light in all things, that which burns in all things.*

Merton's language of burning may also be another way of speaking about encountering Love. As you enter into the silence, and as you take time to do so throughout the day, even if only for brief moments, nurture the fire that burns in all of us and in all creation.

Breathe

Breath in me breathe!
Breathe deeply into silence.
Whisper in the deepest stillness...
Echo there the breath again.
Spirit moves compelling movement.
Spirit stills as movement ceases.
Breath in me breathe!
Be still – be still and know.

Poem from a Place of Silence

The silence of this place calls me to awaken!
Night sky sees with twinkling eye
    fifteen billion ages old.
What does it see, looking as I look back in wonder:
    Itself, and all one in the looking.
Grasses, ferns, leaves, trees sway to silent breath
    of unseen breeze – when it arises I feel it upon my face –
What does it feel, feeling as I do, sitting in this presence –
    Itself and all one in the feeling
The silence of this place
    punctuated with birdsong, buzz of bee, insect chirp –
What does it hear, hearing as I do
    listening in this sounding silence:
    Itself and all one in the hearing.
The silence of this place
    delicious with taste of ancient earth
    and red-ripe berry –
What does it taste, tasting as I do
    the sweetness of this solitude:
    Itself and all one in the tasting.
The silence of this place
    of summer warmth borne on lazy air.
    What does it smell, smelling as I do
    sweetness of honeysuckle released:
    Itself and all one in the smelling.
The silence of this place … yes
    this vast and empty silence
    forever ancient, ever new:
Now, only This Now, calls me to awaken.

Don't Cling

Don't cling – don't cling to this place
   its silence or its grace. Be present
   in each moment holding it as sacred space.
But why O Ground of Being … why can't I call this home?
You said that you would follow blind –
   now come away alone.
Cling not to light or darkness.
Cling not to sight or sound.
In the sea of emptiness
   all life might there abound.
Cling not to life or emptiness
and everything dismiss.
There in depth of silence find
Mystery's silent bliss.

For Reflection: Breath

Along with all living beings, the only thing we do all the time is breathe. Breathing is so much what we do that it is very easy not to think about breath or breathing. In fact, it's easy to take breath for granted. What is the significance of breath?

In the Hebrew Scriptures the word *ruach* means wind, breath, spirit: God breathes life into all living beings, sustains all beings, is a mighty wind. Spirit hovers over chaos.

In the Christian Scriptures there are many references to Breath as Spirit. Jesus told Nicodemus, "The wind blows wherever it pleases. You hear its sound, but you cannot tell where it comes from or where it is going. So, it is with everyone born of the Spirit." (John 3:8) Jesus breathed on his disciples after he was resurrected, giving them the gift of the Holy Spirit. (John 20:22) "And suddenly there came a sound from heaven as of a rushing mighty wind." (Acts 2:2) Jesus was full of the Holy Spirit. (Luke 4)

In the Buddhist tradition of Breath Meditation, "One who has gradually practiced, Developed and brought to perfection, Mindfulness of the in-and-out breath, As taught by the Enlightened One, Illuminates the entire world, Like the moon when freed from clouds." (Theragatha 548) "Breathing in, I calm my body and mind. Breathing out, I smile. Dwelling in the present moment I know this is the only moment." (Thích Nhất Hạnh)

"Prayer is nothing but breathing in and breathing out, the one breath of the universe." Hildegard of Bingen

Consciously stopping to take a few moments of deep breathing in times of anxiety or stress can help restore inner calm and centeredness. Attention to the in-and-out breath in meditation can draw us into a place of centeredness. This helps us to be grounded, present, aware, and awake.

As you prepare to meditate, take a few minutes to reflect on the power of breath, the meaning of *ruach*, the breath-connection with the whole of the universe. Honor and give gratitude for the infinite, mysterious presence of Spirit within, above, over, around, below all that is, and know in each breath that all is One Breath of Love.

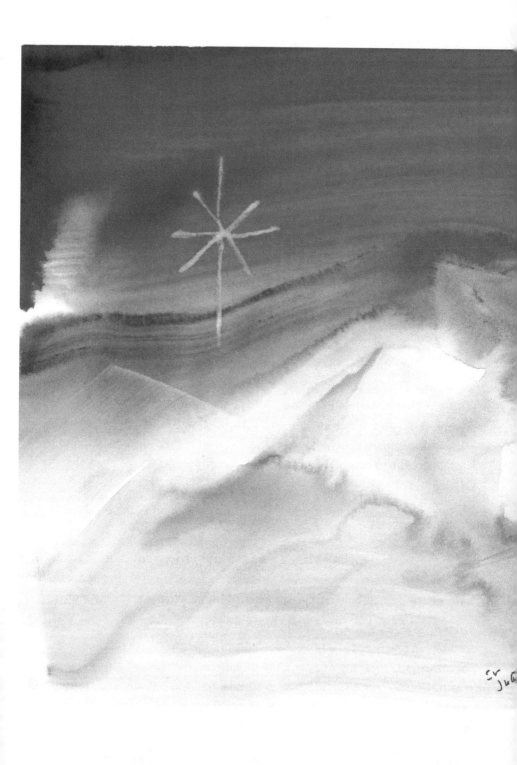

Within Darkness-Infused Light

Watch the wakening of a day ... or a darkening into night. Shapes in ghostly fashion show or sink to shadows in their flight. Mystery, beyond our understanding yet revealed in both shadow and in shape.

Flame of love pierces darkness
Filling all with fleeting light ...
Just as quickly dark returns
One glimpse fleeting bright

      Filled with soft light:
      The quiet Zendo –
      The empty hand.

The winding path –
Light, shadow
And the evening breeze.

Empty Yet Filled

Oh sweetness of an empty darkness
where no eye can see, no touch, no sound.
Old ways crumble, fall and stumble
a new way yet in search not found.
Oh Mystery, Mystery, Mystery
grown cold in dark unknowing
yet smoldering Fire that's fueled in doubt.
Through Shadows a glimmer within the dark.
Deeper, clearer, more simple.
Simple, deeper, clearer.
The pure cloud fades to bright blue sky
before my very eye!

Just Sitting

I sit in darkness not hearing
not seeing. Tongue dry as dust!
No taste to please the palate – only silence!
Lifted on this silent wave
cresting to be plunged more deeply into darkness.
Silence! Like knife's sharp edge
on fresh-baked bread – cuts … cuts
exposing soft flesh beneath its hardened crust.
To what end … to what end these words?
Just look beyond the darkness into
darkened light.

Let Go ... Let Go

The Ground of God is
      the ground of me ...
      of you ... of all that is ...
      that is yet to be.
There is no ground!
      There is no me ... no you ...
      no things here or yet to be.
There is no God for me to see.
Beyond no God,
      beyond no ground ...
      in no-thing all things are found.
Profound is peace ...
      Profound is grace ...
      The eye is clear ...
      All things abound.

At Home

Sometimes I wonder where I am
as I ponder the paths life lays out for me --
Some measured like squares on a chess board,
where each move is made with calculated intent.
Some free flight like bird aloft on waft
of summer breezes.
Some are shaded paths of quiet silence
when my eye turns inward to a secret place.
In this familiar darkness there is an imperceptible light --
something or someone or some place that is known
but cannot be named.
And yet, in this wordless space I know that I am home.

For Reflection: We Wander in Faith

Hildegard of Bingen describes, and I would say defines, prayer as "Breathing in and breathing out the one breath of the universe." Add to that the lovely assertion of Meister Eckhart and so many other saints and sages: "If the only prayer ever said is thank you it would be enough."

Take a few minutes before sitting this evening to step out your door into the briskness of the coming evening. Look up at the evening sky, vastness that it is, search for the stars, or realize the setting of the sun and imagine. Be drawn into, for even a moment, the wonder of this constantly creating, recreating universe. Breathe in and breathe out, whisper to yourself, "the one breath of the universe." Jesus tells us in so many ways that we are not separate from, but rather, one with him, one in the Infinite Mystery, which many name God. The Buddha also experienced and expressed the oneness of all beings.

So many great spiritual teachers tell us again and again, "Know your true self; you are already what you seek." It is for us to come to know, really know, this Mystery and to experience it in brief moments, or sometimes longer moments of realization, and sometimes this means we wander in faith. Maybe we even sense a darkness that seems to hide that Mystery from us. No matter! Breathing in and breathing out the one breath of the universe. See through the darkness the light sitting in light. Know without knowing that It is so.

Be Still

Blinded by the silence of a moonless night
I wander … step by step upon uncharted path
unafraid to let the darkness take me.
Somewhere a beamless light, darkly seen
moves motionless…
beckoning to follow further into night.
A heart cry breaks: Oh where am I!
I AM – be still – in silence I await
your coming within … within
The silence of a moonless dark:
Seek not the dark, seek not the light.
Be still! Be Still! … and see.

Forge and Fire

Flooded, filled, emptied, stilled:
Honey taste of grace-gift Love.
Opened wide to rushing tide –
rest secure on darkened shore.

Wisp of gossamer dims clear light
yet graced a glimpse in whispered breeze.
Flooded, filled, emptied, stilled:
Darkened Light of grace-gift Love.

Smoldering coals are fanned to flame
fired to fullness, emptied, stilled:
burning touch of grace-gift Love
lived as tryst in secret place.

Borne on wing of grace-gift Love –
lifted up beyond all thought.
Flooded, filled, emptied, stilled:
Brought to rest in silent place.

O Living flame – both Forge and Fire
Consume the heart in grace-gift Love.
Flooded, filled, emptied, stilled:
Fire that fashions – Fire that lives.

Flooded, filled, emptied, stilled:
Honey taste of grace-gift Love.
Open wide to rushing tide –
Rest secure on darkened shore.

What Is

Emptiness to fullness filling
but to empty out again –
Darkness to light becoming
but to darkness yet returning.
With blind eye seeing ...
and deaf ear hearing: Knowing
surely All is Well

For Reflection: Light Sitting in Light

Several years ago, when I was in Toronto to participate in a Zen session, I had the good fortune to meet Sister Elaine MacInnes of Our Lady's Missionaries. Sister Elaine was a Zen teacher, and the first Canadian authorized to teach it. On one of my visits, she told me that during a Zen Sesshin[1] she made with her teacher, Zen Master Yamada Kōun Roshi, she asked, "What is prayer for the Buddhist?" Yamada Roshi responded, "It is the same as for the Christian. It is light sitting in light."

As I was reflecting on this simple, profound description of prayer, I was reminded of an eight-year-old boy who, when asked by his religion teacher to draw a picture of God, sat looking at his paper and crayons. After a bit of time, he went to the teacher and quietly said, "I can't draw a picture of God." His teacher asked, "Why not?" He smiled and said, "Because God is light, and you can't draw a picture of light!"

Saints, sages and little children – those with clear eyes and open, uncluttered hearts know without knowing that we, too, are Light! Know when shadows gather and darkness would overtake, light shines through the darkness.

The winding path—
Light, shadow
And the evening breeze.

Wave of light
A touch of warmth
Darkness comes again and all is still.

---

[1] A Zen sesshin in an intensive meditation retreat in a Zen monastery.

Mountains and Hikes

Mountains are a restless rising, some in the wake of glacier flows, some eruptions spewing lava flow. Many snow-clad beaconing the ski and snowshoe. Others barren peaks of solid granite enticing climbers to touch a face of stone. Still others a mix of rock and forest shaded and alluring, teasing come hike the trails to lakes and quiet spots. All the handiwork of Mystery ever ancient ever new.

A winding trail
light, shadow
and the evening breeze

Chill wind sweeps the hills,
dusk turns to darkness
A cold night has come

In shadow of the mountain
tiny flowers grow
earth is renewed again in hope

Hike In a Wooded Place

Tree timbers take notice of the gentle breeze
and groan as if to say:
Notice me! I'm heir to 1000 years of wisdom.
Do not pass me by without at least acknowledgement.
And laughing, dancing falls of water
now quiet, now raucous over rock and log,
making way but taking no notice of the distance
to the mightier stream whose voice swells and cries while
tripping, tumbling toward unknown destination.
Grey mold on the ground speaks of winter's life and death
as tiny buds and dainty flowers make way to spring's new life,
watered by the weight of death in winter snows.
Bright single sunray catches glimpse of dainty branch,
lace-like in the sturdier taller trunk
which bears its tiny weight. It dances in the
whispering breeze and makes ready for the shroud of night.
A hush draws upon the forest – a stillness unmarred
by any noise, save the evensong
of tiny bird, soft distant herald of the coming dark:
To sleep … to silence … to rise and Live.

A Mountain Speaks

Mountain, seething – angry from
your long years sleep awakened
by some mysterious undulating
force deep hidden in molten part.

What calls you now to burst your
rage upon this place?
To speak with thunderous voice
the secrets of your heart?

My feet have climbed the many shapes
that to your crest have led.
Is it nails of many boots which your icy
sides have pierced? Or ropes
which have bit with
careless heed across your sunny face?

Has our world so callous been
with weapons, war and word?
Have we with such irreverence exploited
earth's great heart
and clutched to bosoms, bound
with greed those things not rightly ours?
Is this what calls you angry from
graceful presence shook
to speak with cloud of molten rage
a message of such power?

Ashes out upon this land with mighty
force you spew --
warning to the human heart
that penance will be done.
A call to know a wakefulness to
hold with reverent awe the treasures of our earth,
to share a vision with your heart
of peace that's there to birth.

Yearning for What

My heart yearns for those quiet places
'neath shadow of a mountain
where years have gripped the growing trees,
twisting them to bent and wondrous shapes.
To hear the wind – a gentle, sometimes mighty
voice along the ridge,
beckoning to distances far beyond the
reach of human eye.
It comes and goes as though in haunting
dance that calls to following.
To feel the pulse of Mother Earth
yielding myriads of tiny flowers,
sudden jewels come upon in hidden places …
scented fragrance too rich to bear a name.
To know the strength of rivers, dancing to the sea,
weaving in and out, tripping, tumbling in
journey marked by measured course
upon its mother's brow.
To wonder in the darkened night
of diamond-studded sky,
resplendent with a twinkling light
so hidden in the light of day.
What hand has done this – shaped it all
and placed it here to see?
A loving God, delighted in *His* thought …
Her laughter makes it be.

For Reflection: The Zen of Mary Oliver

During a Zoom Zen Sesshin led by Zen Master Rubén Hábito, he began by saying, "Today, I want to talk about the Zen of Mary Oliver as entering into the realm of the totality of oneness."

In Mary's poem "Sometimes" there is a verse that reads as follows:

Instructions for living a life:
Pay attention.
Be astonished.
Tell about it.

That verse in its entirety contains the whole of Zen practice and through it coming to a realization of the Oneness of all being. *Pay attention. Be astonished. Tell about it.*

Pay attention: Living life in a way that enables us to live from the core of our being, knowing a sense of presence and attention, being present in the here and now, and living fully the present moment.

Be astonished: See! Listen! Be astonished! In her poem "Praying," Mary Oliver invites such astonishment: "It doesn't have to be, the blue iris, it could be, weeds in a vacant lot, or a few, small stones." Find astonishment in everything, everywhere. Everything is a doorway into gratitude, gratitude for everything just as it is.

Pay attention! Zen is a life of paying attention! Mary Oliver so often describes her experience of unfettered happiness, a sense of oneness with the whole universe, the suddenness of realizing the citizenship of all beings in this wonderful world. She is surprised by joy, a sudden impact, a seizure of happiness.

Look into your own life: Ask yourself, "Where do I see or notice things just as they are? Where do I see beauty and goodness? Where do I experience those moments of joy, seizures of happiness in the moment?" Richard Rohr says it well in his book *Everything Belongs: The Gift of Contemplative Prayer:* "I belong, a gift in and to all. Be yourself just as you are."

Tell about it! Live fully present to each moment, present to everything, anywhere, at any time, live the astonishment! Tell about it so others can see and be astonished.

Live life just as you are, manifest your true self! Mary Oliver begins her poem, "Messenger" with the line, "My work is loving the world." Keep your mind on what matters. Our work is to be astonished at what is! Rejoice and be true to the call of infinity. Stand still and notice.

Awesome Wonder Speaks

An eerie blackness moves across the earth:
somber, solemn shroud from unknown source
pulled with awesome slowness by an unseen hand
to steal brightness from warm-lit summer sky.
Stillness settles as silent as the dark is black.

Creatures of the sky their playful songs have ceased
as all nature struck with awe, sentry-silent –
waiting sound from far off place.
And wind whispers cautiously to the
slow approaching eerie dark.

Then even wind-whisper stills,
heaviness enshrouds a wondering land.
Stifling, sultry, sullen ... swollen to
extinguish light –
this somber specter settles, primordial
in its eeriness
and silence of the awestruck becomes
silence of the dead!

What after the dread of mountain's fall?
There comes the
deep-down fresh and gentle tears of God
to wash with wetness parched yet living sod,
and cleanse away ashes of a mountain's fiery mourning
lifting earth from penance to God's promise
of new life borning.

Wind's tender kiss has dried the fresh dropped tears –
picking up each branch and blade as if
with playfulness to ease all trace of haunting fears.
Flowers seem the brighter, their time of penance done
and wait with anxious nodding the warmth
of summer sun.

An Autumn Hike in Cathedral Park

I hiked alone today, the stillness
broken only by the sound of bird,
of grasses moved to rustle by a quiet breeze and
the sound of my own boot upon
the hardened path.
I mused upon the wonder that
confronts my eye and touches the
center of my heart. These I share:

Trunks and limbs of trees
stripped and white lay
strewn like bones from some
ancient grave upturned,
left exposed to weather's forces
that make them whiter still.

Shadows cast by autumn sun
from trees still standing like
silent sentinels above the whitened bones.
Their shadows lengthen
enfolding in their darkening path
grasses — flowers
warming in autumn's call to
winter's seeming death.

Rust-red leaves of tiny shrubs
hug tightly to rock-strewn,
dried up breast of this good earth.
And skirts of spruce trees
turned up, a green-brimmed
cup ready to receive the winter snows.

The sun's hand, alive with diamonds
and black onyx, spreads
them lavishly upon a jade-green lake.
A splendid dance ensues,
sparkling to and fro, up and down,
back and forth in time and rhythm
changing with the touch of wind or breeze.

A pungent perfume, cinnamon-like and rich
hangs heavy in the still, crisp autumn air,
its smell that of summer's blossom
anticipating grip of winter's quiet death.

There is no sadness though in death's
approach. Seasons one upon the other,
year upon myriad of years...
death decays ... life rebirths:
One creation ... One truth ... and
somehow nature knows it!

Then, unbidden, pungent perfume
cinnamon-like and rich rises again
from duff-strewn path – a tempting smell
drawing me to reverie beyond all thought.
A gentle breeze and evening sun invites me to sit a while to ask:
What lessons have I learned, what insights have I gleaned
as I walked this day alone?
One Creation ... One Truth ... One Beauty – Not Two --
somehow Nature knows it.
And if I still my heart to silence ... listen to its deepest song
I know it too!

Hardened Breath

Lava, hardened breath of mountain
   spewed out centuries ago –
Atop, ghostly trees seeking deep for water
   Unavailable and so they die …
standing now as sentinels to what is yet to come.
Pine trees, sheared and chastened
   in harshness of wind and snow –
stand, silent-whitened sentinels
   above a clear blue lake.

For Reflection: Cultivating a Compassionate Heart

It has been said that contemplative/meditative practice opens in a person a deepening sense of compassion. Mindfulness, another contemplative/meditative practice inviting one to live, to be in the present moment, also nourishes compassionate heart. Compassion is active.

We don't need a reminder to know that these are trying, sometimes even scary, times in our world, our country, our cities, and our communities. Compassion and care of and for each other is never more important than in such times. We are asked to be "care-full"—full of care: for ourselves, our families, colleagues, and those we pass on the street or in the supermarket, looking on each of our brothers and sisters, and all of creation with compassion.

A compassionate heart is a loving heart; compassion is love in action. And when we might feel the stress and strain of the tragedies that are so real, it's good to pause and look at the promise of new life and hope in the many who give of themselves to works of mercy and compassion, big and small. A cup of water, a word of support, a lift to the store, a listening ear and heart, there are so many ways of care. It's also a time to pause and take in the beauty that surrounds us, a bright yellow daffodil, the promising bud or the coming-to-life of leaves on a tree. Take in the beauty and serenity of a sunset or sunrise and know in your heart of hearts that life and hope exist in the midst of what seems hopeless.

Compassion is different from empathy; it engages the desire to alleviate the suffering of others. The compassionate person, one whose heart is filled with compassion, is described or defined in many ways and in most religious/spiritual traditions. Here are some of them:

To suffer together

Love in action

To alleviate the suffering of another

Ahimsa: Loving kindness toward all living beings (Hinduism)

Mercy and compassion are two brothers (Islam)

The heart that trembles in the sufferings of another – for all beings to be free from suffering (Buddhism)

Moving the compassionate heart to alleviate – do something to relieve the suffering of another – be compassionate as God is compassionate (Judaism)

Having a heart for those in misery … works at his or her own cost for the others' good, helping to rescue from danger as well as alleviate their suffering. (Christianity)

Be merciful and compassionate as God is merciful and compassionate.

What if every human being throughout our wounded, yet wonderful world exercised mercy and compassion in its fullness – what would our world be like? But really, I can only look to my own heart and wonder what arises in me in the face of human suffering, of earth suffering, of all living beings suffering. What am I called/moved to do? How am I called to be in small, not so small, and maybe sometimes in big ways, or even very big ways to reach out, to suffer with, to alleviate and console, to grieve with, or to lift up one in whom I meet suffering, injustice, hopelessness, or hurt? How am I called to live Love in action? And in the midst of it all, how am I called to be compassionate with myself as well? Perhaps, like praying thanks for all, I would do well to also pray for a loving and compassionate heart … and the wisdom to give it expression.

Beyond All Galaxies

Death is not a single moment, yet we often think of it as that one moment when the thin veil between time and timelessness is parted. If we ponder the mystery of death, we come to realize that really, we 'die' a little each moment of each day. Leaving this good earth, leaving our companions on this journey, stepping through the veil separating time and timelessness is not really an ending but a mysterious return to where we came from: a return to the Ground of All Being – the fullness of life in the Great Mystery we name by many names (God; Infinite Absolute; Source of Life).

Flowers in this vase wither --
their life is but a moment.
Who is it that is dying?
As they are so am I.

      Brown earth
      under decaying leaves.
      And through it white
      snow bells bloom.

Snow falls
A sunflower bends
Leaves heavy with frozen water
The grass must rest awhile.

When Breath Stills

Breath in me breathe!
Breathe deeply into silence.
Whisper in the deepest stillness –
echo there the Breath again.
Spirit moves compelling movement;
Spirit stills and movements cease.
Breath in me has ceased its whisper.
Silence yields to radiant light …
Be still! Be still! And know:
Life is not ended only changed.
Timeless now -- light sits in Light.

Letting Go

Meditation in the Japanese Garden
What must I let go of? — Everything!
But what will happen? Will I disappear and be no more?
Perhaps but not so!
I have let go of images of God – there are none – no image of
the great unknown Mystery.
Yet I realize today in the solitude and silence of a mysterious
space ... I realize a humbling thing:
I have not let go of images of myself! And so I make a 'god'
where no god should be!
What image of self ... of I that will not bend? Image of success
or failure ... of strengths and weakness...
of reality or perception ... of appearance and of fact: of image
so subtle as to blind the inner eye and make noise in the inner
silence – to block the light with unholy darkness – not the
darkness of clear unknowing. Just as I don't know image of
God, I realize that I must come to not-knowing of that subtle
and seductive 'I' (ego/that false self) – only in the unknowing
... the non-knowing of 'I' will the false god fall and True
Essence bubble forth wisdom and compassion ... and even
those fade away! What must I let go of – Everything!

Death Comes

Death comes when? Death comes how?
I don't really know nor can I measure; but now I live!
My breath drawn in and out moment after moment
mostly without thinking – what a gift this is!
Know this my heart:
One day it will be -- the Great Mystery I name Love
will whisper 'Come!' Drawing my very breath back into Itself –
and in that instant life becomes eternity. Death is not an ending,
rather it is a passing into! Life into Life --
What a gift this is!

For Reflection: Letting Go of Expectation

... desire for the Dharma had ensnared my mind and stood in the way of enlightenment.
Zen Master Musō Soseki

... You need seek God neither below or above. God is no further away than the door of the heart.
Meister Eckhart

... we must let go even of God so God can be God in us ... and let God be God in you ... God is at home, It's we who have gone out for a walk.
Meister Eckhart

The quotes above assert the same message for those entering into contemplative prayer or wordless meditation. The first, from Zen Master Musō, was his realization that clinging to the expectations he placed upon his practice of meditation—his wishes for, or thoughts about, or images of how he would be when *enlightened* were the very things that stood in the way of enlightenment.

The others from Meister Eckhart tell us that setting expectations, clinging to thoughts about what we will achieve, and marking progress in contemplation/meditation stand in the way of God's working in the silence of the heart. Therefore, we must let go even of God, so God is free in us.

As you enter into the silence, sitting alone or together in a group, do so with all your heart. Be open and receptive, let go of thoughts, and when they arise, as they will, recognize them and gently let them go, and come back to the silence of your heart. When you find yourself nodding off or wandering in images, gently return to your breath, always coming back to the silence of your heart.

Bring your whole self to this sacred time. Be still in these moments of sacred space, sacred time. Be present, open and awake – neither clinging to nor rejecting anything. Recognize and acknowledge the interruptions that mind or body might present, gently let them go, return to your breath, and come back to the silence of your heart.

As you breathe into the silence of your heart, find there the healing, compassionate presence that touches the joys, sorrows, suffering, and hopes of all. The silence of the heart in the presence of Love imperceptibly transforms far beyond our little space. The Mystery of Love bursts out in compassion. Every extraordinarily ordinary moment, each encounter with another, each hand outstretched to another, each heartbreak over injustice, each word of hope makes this little space of ours, and our wonderful, wounded world, more whole.

Breathe deeply into the silence of your heart and know there, without knowing, the Mystery beyond comprehension: the Ground of God, your true self.

Eternity

Amidst the silent issue of the night
while stars and moon to earth do bend
to caress with gentle light and glow
the creatures that in stillness
answer back in quiet shadow...
there beats with slow, uneven strain,
rhythmed only by rise and fall of tide
the restlessness of created thing
held in patient waiting
only by the strings of time.
The silent stillness pulsing through
the veins of Mother Earth, unhurried,
yet with ever quickening beat
toward the time when time shall be no more
and broken be the cords that bound
us to the march of years --
the dawn of glory dimly on the line,
becoming brighter as each minute speeds its course onward
toward the brightness of the orb of day that kindles
life and warmth...
bringing to full growth the one that
so short a span ago in restless stillness lay.
And then with force made gentle beyond
the power of the mind to fully grasp,
ties that bound are broken and released
that one to be caught up in
blaze of burning day where time has
met with endlessness and thus become Eternity.

How Will It Be

How will it be between us
now that you are there and I am left behind?
Or is there any in between?
I would like to think not … rather to know
that now our spirits merge as one
and are indivisible … not bound by barrier of
time or matter. Yes I would rather know that
each breath drawn in draws you into
the inner reaches of my heart and there we are
more than ever one in that ancient sacred art of breathing
in the great Mystery of the Spirit's whispering presence.

If I listen with my heart will I hear you
in the whisper of the gentle breeze?
In the rushing wind through branches
of trees you loved so well? Will I see
your smile in the purple pansy as it
looks up at me? Or in the red geranium
drawing to itself the tiny humming bird?
Your laughter in the running water … your gaze upon me
in the morning sun? I want to know these things…
to know you are truly here
in new and wondrous ways just as is the
Great Mystery of the Spirit's whispering presence.

Will I come to know, if I listen silently enough
that death is truly but a parting of the thin
veil which for a time keeps us here … that when
death draws us into parting there is a freedom
and fullness beyond all limits … a freedom that
defies illusion of time and space, knowing now
unfettered movement of the Spirit's whispering presence.
Will I come to know, if I listen silently enough? This is my hope.

How will it be between us
now that you are there and I am left behind?
Or is there any 'in between'?
Take my hand, touch my heart and show me.

Tokoji Temple

To walk among the dead
and know no fear
surrounded by the living
in leaf and song
The Ancient One speaks
a word that is true
ringing like silence
fresh as morning dew
I don't know whose grave
I sit beside —
But know we are one:
the same inside.

Let me respectfully remind you
Life and death are of supreme importance
Time swiftly passes and opportunity is lost.
Each of us should strive to awaken...awaken!
Take heed! This night your days are diminished by one.
Do not squander your life.

Chant recited each evening in most Zen meditation groups.

For Reflection: We Are One

How important it is to remember that we are all one—not separate from those who are well, those who are ill, those who are joyful, those who are anxious, those who are homeless, and those caught in the horror of an unprovoked war in Ukraine. Know without knowing that what happens to one, to the earth, to all beings, happens to you and to me.

Breathe deeply into the silence, knowing that we are one in the Ground of All Being. We sit together in the midst of human suffering and weep, in the midst of human joy and rejoice, in the midst of all creation and give thanks. Clearly Love's tears are the same as those that wash our own eyes and soften our hearts. Love's laughter invites us to rejoice. Love's beauty offers hope and healing. Even though it may seem long in coming, Julian of Norwich reminds us, "All shall be well, and all shall be well, and all manner of things shall be well, for there is a force of Love moving through the universe that holds us fast and will never let us go."

Opening to a Mystery beyond our comprehension imperceptibly transforms the human heart leading us to new and deeper ways of seeing and being present to the extraordinarily ordinary experiences of our everyday living and being. This is expressed in this excerpt from Evelyn Underhill's *The Spiritual Life.*

> *That means trying to see things, persons and choices from the angle of eternity; and dealing with them as part of the material in which the Spirit works. This will be decisive for the way we behave as to our personal, social, and national obligations. It will decide the papers we read, the movements we support, the kind of administrators we vote for, our attitude to social and international justice. For though we may renounce the world for ourselves...we have to accept it as the sphere in which we are to co-operate with the Spirit...*

and try to express Love's compassionate care of and presence in all.

The ground is holy on which we walk,
In which we stand and are absorbed.
Reach out beyond the stillness there
To hear the opening of a door.

Epilogue

Each person's journey is uniquely shaped yet common in the restless longings of the human heart to touch, to feel, to hear, to taste the *Infinite Mystery* called by many names, none of which ever fully describes what can only be experienced, and so the need for simile and metaphor. Poetry rises in the heart and finds expression in words that only in small ways describe 'what is' for each of us. Let yourself give voice to what rises in you as you find yourself in moments of solitude and silence, or on bustling streets and busy places, or when you are just walking around and Mystery brushes up against you ... or meets you face to face. Let feeble words give expression in whatever form they come.

About Kenmare Press

Kenmare Press is an imprint of the Sisters of St. Joseph of Peace. In accord with our tradition and the spirit of our founder, Margaret Anna Cusack (Mother Francis Clare), we launched this publishing project in 2019, our 135th anniversary year. Mother Clare was herself a prolific writer, most often publishing as M.F. Cusack or Mary Francis Cusack. By 1870, more than 200,000 copies of her works had circulated throughout the world. Profits from the sale of her books were used for the sisters' work with the poor. Today, many of her books are in the public domain and available to read or download online.

In addition to *Images of Refuge*, we have published other books written by sisters that are available in paperback and eBook format at online booksellers and at csjp.org.

Peace Pays a Price: A Study of Margaret Anna Cusack by Dorothy Vidulich, CSJP

Margaret Anna Cusack was bold, courageous and visionary. She dedicated her life to fighting social injustice, especially toward the poor and woman and children.

Based on Cusack's many books, biographies, letters and other research, Sister Dorothy Vidulich has written a concise study of Cusack's life. In particular, she has focused on Cusack's courage to confront the discrimination and injustice promulgated by society and a patriarchal church, which ultimately forced her to leave the religious order she had founded for it to be saved.

Traveling Empty: Poems by Susan Dewitt, CSJP

This collection of poems from Sister Susan Dewitt invites the reader on a holy journey through kitchens and gardens, women's shelters and desert retreat centers and beyond. From the opening poem "Breath by Breath" beseeching Spirit to provide ailing lungs with a few more million breaths to the closing "Blessing for Quinn" wishing a grandniece a world of natural beauty into the future, these works evoke the sacred.

My Friend Joe: Reflections on St. Joseph by Susan Rose Francois, CSJP

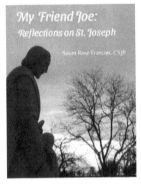

St. Joseph, husband of Mary and foster-father of Jesus, is central to the Christian story. Yet, so little is known about him either as an historical figure or as recorded in scripture. Much of what we understand about Joseph comes to us from tradition, art, and the lived experience of the faithful over the centuries.

Inspired by photographs of Joseph that she's taken, Sister Susan Rose Francois reflects on her growing spiritual friendship with St. Joseph, whom she affectionately calls her friend Joe. Through art, prose, history, and prayer she encourages the reader to discover, or deepen, their own spiritual friendship with St. Joseph

Images of Refuge by Margaret Jane Kling, CSJP

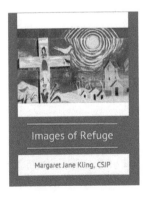

This collection of letters and documents records the period of time that Sister Margaret Jane Kling, Sister Andrea Nenzel, and others served in El Salvador with the Jesuit Refugee Service, living and working with refugees in San José Calle Real. A remarkable historical record that highlights how little has changed for refugees in war-torn countries.